Table Of Contents

Like then Share!

Click to share a free copy with your Facebook friends

(Don't worry, it won't auto share!)

About The Author

 Michael Amerson

A longtime resident of Las Vegas, Nevada, Michael Amerson is a video game developer, who has worn many hats. In his 12-year career, Mike has been a 2D, 3D and lead artist, animator, web developer, project manager, designer, creative director, business development, and marketer. Mike has 10 published video game titles to date, including credits on mega hits such as: Star Wars — Empire at War and Call of Duty — World at War.

In 2009 Mike Ventured into iOS space as Co-founder and President of WET Productions Inc. Just a year later, in 2010, he released the hit iOS game My Virtual Girlfriend, whose launch was featured on MSNBC, Kotaku, and the late night TV show Lopez Tonight! with comedian George Lopez. Mike later followed up to that title with the partner iOS game My Virtual Boyfriend, which was featured in an article on TechCrunch.

Introduction

WET Productions, Inc.

My name is <u>Mike Amerson</u>. I'm the President of WET Productions, Inc., and the co-creator of the app games <u>My Virtual Girlfriend</u> and <u>My Virtual Boyfriend</u>. WET Productions is an independent virtual studio comprised of two guys working out of our homes, separated geographically by different continents. We rely on technology and discipline to run our business, as my partner and I have never actually met in person. We established our relationship eight years ago after meeting in a game development forum.

After collaborating on a few ideas together, we eventually grew into a video game development business — all through the Internet. Our first published game, *My Virtual Girlfriend*, was released for iPhone in May of 2010. It went from making $15.00 a day to $900.00 per day, hitting many price points in between. Our paid version currently averages about 150 downloads per day, and on weekends it can spike up to 250 downloads per day; our recently released *My Virtual Boyfriend* does about the same. We haven't localized the game yet, so our focus is marketing to English-speaking countries such as the US, UK, and Canada.

While sales have generally declined over time, we work proactively to sustain the business with several techniques, which I've outlined in this book. I wrote this because I wish to share with you some insights that I've learned and what you can expect, in the hope that it may bring you closer to success with your game.

Chapter 1: Getting Started

Background

I've been in video game development for over 10 years, during which time I've learned that traditional game development for both PC and console requires significant marketing efforts in order for it to become commercially successful. These marketing efforts are generally proportionate to the development cost: the bigger the title, the more money is spent to ensure it receives proper exposure. (It would be a huge risk for publishers not to do so!) When a console game is released, it usually has a shelf life of only 6–12 months for a good game, so the marketing department will work to aggressively promote it during that time by focusing the majority of their marketing efforts at launch.

In iOS app marketing, you'll find a similar system in play. The launch of your app is considered to be the most crucial part, and is where you should do your biggest marketing push. However, if you're an indie developer like me, you are probably your own marketing team, so you'll need to do much of the work yourself. The good news is that this book will help you by providing you with a deep understanding of what's involved, and pointing you to the proper resources to help you out. Drawing upon my own personal experience, this ebook details how to propel your games into top spots in the iTunes app store, and maintain them. Like anything else in life, once you get the hang of it, it's not so difficult, but it does require you stay current with this ever-evolving landscape. In the end it's all about managing your resources, testing, and applying what you've learned.

Development costs for an iPhone app can range from $3,000 to $500,000. The shelf life of an app isn't subject to the same rules as PC or console games. An engaging app will sustain high rankings in the app store. Just look at Tetris or NBA Jam—these games are over 15 years old, but have built a reputation on being fun and engaging, and continue to deliver. As a result, since being ported over to the iPhone, they remain chart-toppers.

So if your game proves its worth, you should work to update it with new and improved content whenever possible. Listen to what the players want by reading their reviews, and work hard to accommodate their requests. If you do this and the result improves the overall experience, then you're effectively evolving your game over time, and giving it an indefinite shelf life.

According to 148apps.biz, there are over 593,311 apps currently available in the App Store. It is an extremely competitive space that requires both a great app and a solid marketing campaign to be profitable. Just putting your app in the App Store does not guarantee a profit. Customers have to find it first, and for that you need exposure — lots of it.

Considerations

There are many aspects of marketing you'll need to consider: do I need to spend? If so, how much, and for how long? But the biggest consideration is identifying the most efficient and cost-effective methods to gain exposure for your product, (i.e. what produces the biggest bang for the buck). This is the toughest question, and one that doesn't come with a direct answer. It's really about finding which method works best for your game and exploiting that to the fullest.

Understand that the iOS market is a volatile landscape, with new marketing methods available online every day. The challenge here is to stay on top of current events, while sifting the wheat from the chaff. It's a tall order—but not an impossible one. It will simply require you to devote some time and learn a new skill set; but with metrics on our side, we can make proper evaluations while mitigating the risks.

Marketing Costs

I am often asked something along the lines of, "How much should be spent on marketing?" The answer to this will vary from project to project, but one common sense rule applies to all: spend as much as you can on the things that give you a return on investment.

Think of it as a formula. Let's use a ratio of 1:2 as an example, for simplicity. If you have a good game and you spend $500/month, your returns at that ratio would be $1,000/month. By the same token, if you spend $5,000/month, the returns would equate to $10,000/month. Sounds pretty good, right? Just keep in mind that the 1:2 ratio is just an example, and a pretty decent one at that. Anything that offers you more back than your spending is considered to be good. And the higher the quantity you sell, the more leadway you have to turn less of a profit off of an individual sale, so it's ok to have a low profit margin if you're making up for it in quantity.

For example: if you only make $ 0.10 profit off of each app you sell, but you're making 1M sales per month, then you're actually generating $100,000 per month—not a bad deal for an indie developer. However, if you were to price your app to where it makes $3 per sale, but because of the higher price it only get 100 sales per month, then it's probably not the most efficient way for you to monetize. Remember that quantity is king in this game, and the lower price points (including free) tend to get way more downloads than a paid version. In either case, it's ultimately up to you to determine where that profit margin sweet spot is.

Just to give you a starting point, I will reference my own game. For *My Virtual Girlfriend*, I typically spend 10-25% of the previous month's revenues on marketing. That means I'll spend between $500-$1,200/month on marketing (more on the specifics of that spending later).

- The higher amounts account for when I'm about to push a significant update, as there are more costs associated with announcements.
- If it's a launch effort, you will want to come out strong, then try to maintain that pace by re-investing a percentage of your proceeds back into marketing your app.
- If you have a strong launch, but don't gain momentum during the first two weeks, your game will probably not get enough traction and it will fail to gain a top 100 ranking in the App Store for it's primary category, At this point you should really look to examine why it didn't gain traction, and if possible, work toward an update that addresses the biggest player concerns.

Launch Costs

If you're an indie developer or are on a shoestring budget, try to have at least $1,000 at launch as an initial marketing push. This will cover expenses such as:

- The writing and distribution of your press release.
- A promotional video review or demo of your game.
- A few "expedited" (paid reviews) on app websites.
- A couple paid ads for additional exposure.

These are just the minimal marketing costs that you need to pay for—we aren't yet including the grassroots or social marketing efforts you will be doing personally. With these combined efforts, a good product, and a little luck, it may be enough to gain some traction within the App Store. Even so, plan to allocate 10-25% of your profit each month towards next month's marketing budget so you can keep the momentum rolling. Be as aggressive as you comfortably can. Carefully monitor your marketing efforts to see what's giving you good return on investment, and what's not. There are plenty of resources out there that help you to measure metrics and data, (you could try AppFigures or Flurry) but it will require some dedicated effort to monitor and maintain them.

If you are an indie developer, working to create an app on the side apart from your full-time job, and you plan to sustain a career in mobile app development, you will need to treat development as a business. Building the game was only half the battle. Now you must take on research and development, measuring analytics, marketing, staying current with trends, monetization strategies…and all that other biz-dev stuff the exec's claim to do at your day job. But believe me when I say that these roles do, in fact, make up a full day's work.

With any business comes a certain amount of risk, but the rewards can far outweigh the risk—as long as you play your cards right. You just have to put your game face on and come prepared. Here are three keys to success.

1. Create with quality in mind.
2. Engage your users.
3. Exposure, Exposure Exposure!

Chapter 2: Developmental Considerations

Create A High Quality Game/App

Long gone are the days when you can put out a simple novelty app and expect to cash in on it: this might seem obvious to some, but to others it's an eye-opener. In today's market, a mediocre app will get buried by other high-quality apps. If you plan to generate big sales, you must offer something that has value for the consumer—even when the app is only $0.99, or even free, because they are still investing their time, and people value their time.

It also goes hand in hand with your marketing plan. The first thing to do is to create a "high concept," as simple as a 1-2 page document, that identifies key information and serves as the basis for what may later become your design document. (You can find a template later on in this ebook.) Once you have this conceptual base, consider the following:

1. **Target Audience:** Identifying your primary audience will help keep you aligned with making sound development decisions, as well as helping you to craft your marketing plan. Ask yourself these questions about your target audience: Is it primarily male or female? What is the age range? Is it for the casual or hardcore game player? Is it an app for business or the general consumer? For the best results, identify your target audience before development. You can work your way out to include a broader audience from there.

2. **Mass Appeal:** I know a lot of developers will cringe when they hear this, because it's a sentiment commonly despised in the industry. It's also absolutely true: Commercial success is a numbers game. The broader the appeal, the more sales. Creating your *personal* dream app, "Super Shortwave Radio receiver for contact with beings from the planet of Zar" may *not* have broad appeal. So unless you don't mind having only five downloads, save yourself some disappointment and learn to make the distinction between personal and commercial projects.

For my part, I didn't make a game about virtual girlfriends because I have a virtual girl fetish—I made it because I realized there is a market. After seeing the success of simple titles like *Igirl* and *Pocket Girlfriend* in the App Store, I realized there was an audience for this. And while these titles didn't really offer much in terms of gameplay, what they *did* have was novelty and the advantage of being in the app store early on. (I commend the developers for having the foresight and quick response to be among the first to get their apps into the App Store.) That said, I knew I could make something better, and hoped to capitalize on having an app that had the same novel appeal, but with a more gratifying experience.

3. **Be Innovative:** Create something unique or enhance an existing concept. Just cloning a current idea usually proves fruitless. If it's a valid concept, and it's doing well, then the developers of the original idea will have updated their app with new content by the time you're done developing. You will remain one step behind them, because you're perpetually reacting to what they do.

Create a list of reasons why your app stands out, such as game-play features, graphics, sounds, or functions that are unique to your app. This list will help you stay focused on what matters most during development. It calls out any unique features your app may have, which comes in handy during your marketing campaign. And it will also serve as the basis to write your app store copy. It's important that you communicate these items to players quickly and effectively: you only have their attention for just a couple seconds so put your best assets forward.

It's also likely that the players will recognize a knock-off, and will react negatively in your App Store reviews. Plus, you could lose respect from other developers and publishers, and that's one bridge you don't want to burn before you cross it. So keep in mind: be creative, be innovative, and if you feel compelled to develop an app that you are inspired by, expand on that concept and enhance the experience.

Competition

Becoming aware of apps similar to your own will help you to define a strategy, so find and identify the top five apps that are similar to yours. Once you have that list, play through them to discover the "sticky" points that make that game a success. Use this to your advantage in the following ways:

- Read the ratings/reviews in itunes. The players who installed the app will express what they would like to see in the future, as well as complain about what they don't like in the current version. I bet you'll find several of the same suggestions and, by incorporating them into your app, avoid the mistakes of other developers. Customer reviews should be the #1 resource to identify player wants and complaints.

- Find out who's talking about your competition. Use Google Alerts to set up keyword searches that pertain to similar apps. These alerts will send you links to other apps being covered by bloggers and reviewers. These writers probably already have an interest in that subject matter, so you can get in contact with them and ask them to write about your game when the time comes.

- Research their commercial viability. Want to know how well an app does? Check its ranking in iTunes. The lower the ranking, the less likely it is to do well commercially, as there is a direct correlation between app store ranking and sales. Wanna get an estimate of how many sales an app has? Check out xylogic.com — they display stats that appear to be somewhat accurate and give indication to how well a game is doing. Also, if you're doing a Freemium type of game, be sure to check out your competitors top in-app purchases.

One other thing I'd like to mention about "the competition": although you may have similar apps, the developers themselves are NOT your enemy. Don't write negative reviews of competing games just because you think it will give you some advantage and make your game look better. Not only is this bad ethics, it's not practical either. With most games priced at just $0.99, players will most likely buy more than one of that game type because it's something they are already interested in. Think about it: how many physics-based puzzle games or racing games do you have on your iPhone? Probably a few of each.

In fact, a good developer will often reach out to leverage another who has a similar app, and the two will work out some kind of cross-promotion. This is the strategy that bigger app promotional platforms, such as <u>Flurry</u> and <u>Tapjoy</u>, use: they take stats from players and offer suggestions to them based on what they are playing.

The truth is, you're not competing with other developers, or even their apps — you are competing with the *players* for their time and attention. And that attention can be focused on any game in the App Store, since most players don't play just one type of game. The players are the judges: they decide who gets their attention, through criteria based on personal preference. There is no standard, no finish line that determines a winner and loser.

Names Matter

Naming Your App

Remember the dotcom boom of the late 90's, when people were scurrying to buy up domain names because they had "key" words in the title? Well, that's starting to take hold in app development, because developers have learned that—just like in a web search engine—your app's name plays a big role in the store's search engine algorithm and thus its discoverability within the search function.

In fact, it's the **primary** factor. Your app's name should NOT be overlooked.

People will often use the search feature in the App Store to find something they are specifically looking for, such as "bowling" or "enchilada recipes." The apps that pull up to the top of that search list will be the ones that use those actual words in the name of the app. The (100 character) keywords you enter into iTunes connect will also play a part, but they're secondary to the name. If you have a specialty Mexican recipe application, for example, a name like "Best Mexican Recipes" would work. Another would be "Great Mexican Cookbook." Of course, you should try to limit the amount of characters in the title, while still getting a keyword or two in there.

Your Company Name

You may have already have a company name, or one you want to use; if so, that's fine. But consider that the App Store searching algorithm also considers your company name in its search index, and weighs it heavily.

Ever see company names with strange titles and wonder why? Something like "BestCoolFunNakedGirlApps." (This example is fictitious, by the way. But it does demonstrates a point.) A few developers have figured out that using keywords in their company name works to their advantage. In fact, it is believed to be nearly as important as your app title, as far as the App Store search engine is concerned.

Size MAtters

Keeping the file size under 20 MB is a great advantage for developers, because it broadens the audience. Files over 20 MB must be connected to a Wi-Fi source or directly downloaded to a customer's computer before being transferred to the device. If your app has a file size of over 20 MB, it eliminates a significant number of potential customers who are not near a wifi source and are inclined to make a spontaneous purchase or installation.

If your game is inherently large, consider selling a "base" game (sized under 20 MB), and then monetize with in-app purchases to expand on the existing base download. Look at the top 25 games currently in the App Store, and I'm willing to bet that whenever you read this, ninety percent of the top 25 apps will be under 20 MB downloads. Best-sellers (like Angry Birds, Draw Something, Fruit Ninja, Where's My Water, Tiny Wings, Cut the Rope, Bejeweled, Tetris, and Words with Friends) all conform to this rule. Savvy publishers and developers realize the value in accessibility.

In this case of *My Virtual Girlfriend*, I've noticed it will fluctuate in the App Store by 20 places in rank throughout a week. I believe that a portion of this is tied to the fact that people are home on weekends, where they have an Internet connection and can download the app easily. The high ranking the app receives on Sunday gives it significant exposure, which then carries momentum into Monday. Ranking will probably start to die down on Tuesday.

Wednesday, Thursday, and Friday are the week's lowest points. This is because during the work or school day, people will impulsively download apps under 20 MB, which transfer to their phones through their service providers. If an app's file size is over 20 MB, it can't transfer through the service provider, so the person downloading it tells himself that he will wait until he gets home. Unfortunately, the impulse to buy it has usually left him by that time.

The takeaway? Try to keep your file size down to get the impulse installs.

Create A FREE (Try Before You Buy) Version

Many developers fear that a free version will cannibalize their paid version, so they are reluctant to create one. But this is only true if you have a mediocre app. If you offer something unique and entertaining, you'll find that having a free version is actually a huge advantage. Here's why…

First off, a free version will likely get 100 times more downloads than a paid version. Let's use *My Virtual Girlfriend* as an example. When we first launched, we didn't have a free version, and upon launch our paid version averaged around 30 downloads per day. When we came out with the Lite (free) version, we averaged about 3,000 downloads per day on that version.

When this happened, the sales from the paid version shot up to around 300 per day. The free version's sole purpose was to get people to convert to the paid version—so it seemed we had found our magic missile. And our success in this endeavor isn't unique. I've confirmed with other developers who have had similar results.

Secondly, it's important to receive positive feedback in your ratings in the App Store. The best way to filter out negative reviews and comments is by allowing people to try your game before they buy it, so they know what they're getting. This way, they are less likely to be disappointed by finding out the app is not what they thought, and can get a feel for the experience that allows them to make an informed decision when they purchase the full version. This leads to a higher overall ranking for the paid version in the App Store, as people who know what they are getting are less likely to leave a negative review. Thus, the free version serves as a negativity buffer to your paid version.

Keep in mind, however, that a "lite" (essentially a demo) version requires a good balance to be successful. It must be compelling enough to play, but not be so satisfying that the players doesn't want to pay for the full version. Anything over a 2% conversion rate is considered good. The conversion ratio on *My Virtual Girlfriend* is around 10%. This is partly due to the the method I use to up-sell: I entice the player by having the characters suggest—while in-game—that the player buy the full version.

Now, not everyone can do it like that, and most will use a pop-up that explains the benefits of their game with a link to buy the full version. For our game, this is one of more interesting and effective methods we are able to use, without detaching the player from the game environment. The point is that finding a unique way to up-sell using the context of your app is always more refreshing than a simple text message.

Create For All IOS Devices

At first, *My Virtual Girlfriend* targeted only the iPhone and the iPod touch (which count as one device). But later, we decided to make our app universal, so that it worked on the iPad as well, and didn't require a separate download. This nearly doubled our sales, because we were now on two devices. The code didn't require too much reworking for the iPad, so for us it was just a matter of increasing the resolution of the graphics and repositioning some of the UI (User Interface). A third device to consider is the Mac App Store, which allows users to run the app on their PCs.

The downside to making a universal app is that there is no current way to separate iPhone from iPad purchases. (This matters because you may want to know how well a specific platform is doing.) You can track the ranks separately, but when you make a universal app, the sales data is combined. You don't know which platform has a stronger presence, or by what percentage. This means you're missing valuable sales metrics that can influence how you spend your marketing dollars. They also may determine whether you want to develop for a particular platform in the future.

The upside to having a universal app is that there's evidence that it factors into your rankings from one device to another. I've observed that whenever *My Virtual Girlfriend* jumps up or down in rank for a particular country, I get a similar result for the iPad. I've measured these results in an hour-by-hour comparison using app monitoring tool at Appfigures.com.

Social Dynamics Are HUGE

Zynga uses social mechanics to virally communicate the existence of their games, by incorporating game-play that relies on a Facebook user's friends to help him or her achieve goals in the game.

iOS developers are catching on to this too. A social dynamic should be incorporated into game-play whenever possible: not only does it add value to the game, but will help to spread the word by having an avenue through which the consumer does the viral marketing for you.

Here are a few methods of social dynamic that you should consider, in order of priority. Bear in mind that these methods may or may not fit into what you have, and that most of these methods apply to only to games. There are, however, some ideas here that non-game apps can use.

1. **Social Mechanics**: Draw Something is a fantastic example of a social mechanic incorporated into the design of the game. As an integral aspect of the game, you must play with another human being, so virility is amplified. It is reported that Draw Something currently has 38 million installs, and was recently purchased by Zynga for 180 million. To note, a big portion in the valuation of that IP has to do with the amount of users that the game acquired in such a short time — only 6 weeks on the market as of this writing.

   Although not inherit in the design, Zombiebooth 3D also does a good job of adding a social mechanic in order to have the public market the app for them. It allows the user to take a "zombified" photo or video, and to post it to the various social networks like Youtube, Facebook and Twitter. Brilliant! Free, wide-scale exposure.

2. **Multiplayer**: Games that offer a multiplayer option help your game acquire new players through friends of your current users. It also makes for a unique and challenging experience. Playing with or against other humans is generally preferred over playing by onesself for the majority of gamers out there, so whenever possible it's good to give the player this option. A nice example of a top iOS multiplayer game would be NBA Jam, which uses both bluetooth and wifi to play cooperatively and competitively. I would suggest that you consider both methods of engagement.

3. **Challenges:** The uber-successful app <u>Words with Friends</u> did a fantastic job rising to challenges by seamlessly encouraging players to get their friends involved in a one-on-one session. The players encourage their own friends to play, which gets you more users for your game. And since it's turn-based, it doesn't require a lot of advanced server technology.

4. **Social Gaming Networks:** These forums allow players to show off their accomplishments and to see the accomplishments of others. In some cases, the game also provides communication tools to engage with other players directly. They allow players to connect, compete and even earn rewards. They encourage the players to meet new friends and try new games.

   There are a number of popular social gaming networks that developers can utilize, but I would recommend <u>Gamecenter</u>, <u>Open Feint</u>, or <u>Scoreloop</u>. All have a similar feature set, including leaderboards, challenges, and achievements, and each one offers increased exposure through social mechanics.

In the end, these things provide added functionality to your app, give players a community, and provide opportunities for more exposure for your game — potentially to millions of players. Several of the top 10 games, like Angry Birds, Fruit Ninja, and Cut the Rope, incorporate one or more of these because of the advantages they offer.

Monetization

The way your game will generate revenue should be thought about and incorporated early into the app design. It is essential to figure out which strategy works best for the type of game you are creating.

Here are a few common methods of monetization:

1. **A fixed price (aka: "paid" app):** The simplest and most direct model. The user pays a single fixed price for the app with all it has to offer. This is one of the more common approaches because it simply is the easiest to do. It was very common in the early years of the itunes app store. However, as the quantity of apps grew, discoverability became a growing concern of developers whose apps did not have high rankings. Sales were dismal and many a developer would not be able to recoup development costs. Developers had to get more creative and come up with new ways to generate income.

1. **In-app Advertising:** This is where you run advertisements within your app. As players click on them, you earn revenue. You can seek out advertisers manually, but the quickest and most widely accepted route is to go through a <u>mobile marketing platform</u>.

In-app advertising works best if you do this within your free app. I don't recommend putting ads in your paid apps, as users will typically frown on seeing ads in something they have purchased. Since Apple has provided a feedback system for each app, players will not hesitate to leave you a nasty review and a 1-star rating if you choose to include advertisers in a paid app. That being said, it is commonplace to see ads in free apps. The trick to their efficiency is using ads that are relevant to your audience — which is another reason why defining your app's target audience is crucial.

Placement also plays a key role, so be sure the ad is not obtrusive or pushy, or you'll risk loss of user retention and see your ad ratings plummet. A great place for a full-page ad is to have them replace your load screens. This way, they are not detracting from actual gameplay. Also, keep mind that in-app advertising is a numbers game; it always works best if the app has a significant install base.

2. **Free app, with in-app purchases (aka "Freemium"):** Pioneered by the social games market for the PC, the Freemium model is how <u>Zynga</u> grew to be such a powerhouse in

just a few short years.

It is the combination of both science and psychology. The idea behind the Freemium model is that you first establish a large user base by offering the app for free. The players then begin to develop a "stake" in the game by having committed a certain amount of time and energy into it. A little further into the game, the developer will introduce in-app purchases, which will offer something of value for the player. Stakes can be something that gives the player an advantage in completing their goals in the game, or they can be purely aesthetic in nature. Either way, the Freemium model is a great option for developers because of the low barrier to entry for acquiring installs.

Note: According to data provided to VentureBeat, iOS Freemium game apps are generating $14.66 per-user, per-year—more than a paid game without in-app purchases. This is why the Freemium model is growing so rapidly, and is considered to have the highest potential for generating revenue in mobile space.

3. **Paid App With In-app Purchases:** Similar to the Freemium model, this method aims to maximize revenues by charging for the app, as well as using in app purchases to broaden revenue. A great example of this is Halfbrick's Jetpack Joyride. This model works with this game because Halfbrick offers a full game experience for the purchase price, while the in-app purchase items are enhancements; if you never made a purchase through the entire game, it would still be an enjoyable experience. This is the key to making this model work: it is a full game experience that allows for additional content to be acquired, if the players choose to.

The downside to this model is that by putting a price on it up front, you potentially raise the barrier to entry. This model works best on games that offer an outstanding gameplay experience that can be further enhanced through in-app purchases.

A note about piracy: Both the Freemium and Paid with in-app purchase models help to discourage piracy of your app. In a Freemium game, there is no incentive for a pirate to crack an already free game. With in-app purchases, the app has to connect to the iTunes server to download that additional content. Although a pirate may be able to crack an individual app and distribute it among P2P (peer-to-peer) or jailbreak networks, they can't distribute those sub-component, in-app purchasable items, because the items can come directly via download from iTunes and are not be stored within the app client.

Mobile Marketing Platforms (MMP)

Mobile Marketing Platforms (also known as App discovery, Ad network and monetization platforms) are intermediary service providers that have created a system connecting publishers with advertisers. They offer developers the tools to earn revenue as a publisher by advertising other developer's apps across your apps; in this way, you both receive earnings from the installs that occur, and gain an additional channel for user acquisition. In addition to this, many MMP's also offer some analytics through their dashboard, giving stats for your daily active users, what time of the day they play, how often, etc.

Either way, these platforms provide the tools that allow for both promotion and monetization to take place. Here is generalized breakdown of what most of them offer:

- **Advertising:** You can advertise your app across other apps in their network, though the rates for advertising vary. Some have a set price, while others are managed via a bidding system. Both are tracked and measured through clicks or installations of your app. The cost you may pay per click (CPC) or cost per install (CPI) will vary, but is typically around $0.30 CPC and $1.00 CPI. More about the Pay Per Install service here.

- **Publishing:** You can earn revenue by allowing other brands or developers to advertise their product across your apps. In most cases, this will be a revenue sharing split between you and the mobile ad network (who is essentially brokering the deal). One example: For a CPI set at $1 per install, you would get $0.50 per install on a revenue split of 50/50 between you and the ad network.

- **Internal Cross-Promotion:** Some of the MMP's provide you with tools that allow you to create an internal cross promotion campaign. This is usually offered as a free tool within their SDK (Software Developers Kit), which allows you to promote one of your own apps, across your other apps for additional exposure.

Pay-Per-Install

Many MMP's offer a pay-per-install service, where you pay for individual installs that occur on user devices. Essentially, you are advertising your app across other apps and paying for the installs you receive.

The pricing for this service varies, but for most places and it works off a bidding system. The developer can pay anywhere from $0.75 per install to $2.25 per install — and that's on a free game. (The price can be even higher on paid games.)

For most campaigns, the developer will set a budget for how much they are willing to spend on a given campaign. (Note: this is based off of quantity, so prices usually start at $2500 and go up from there.) There is either a silent bid with other developers, or the service will simply charge a flat fee per install. The developer then pays the MMP up front for the installs that are to occur, based on the price that has been set for each installation. The MMP promotes that app across other apps in their network using an in-app advertisement system, resulting in large quantities of installations in little time. This is also known as "burst advertising." All the while, each installation that occurs is being tracked and tallied up. When the budget has run out, the campaign ends.

So why would anyone in their right mind pay for someone to download their free game? The answer isn't obvious to most, but if your app is using the Freemium model to generate revenue, this method can be quite effective, as it is reported that Freemium games make on average $14.00 per install (Source: Flurry Analytics).

In the Freemium model, games and apps typically make an average of around $14.00 in revenue over the lifetime of the app. If a developer spends $1.50 to make $14.00, then he's making $12.50 in profit per installation. Not only does this method generate revenues, it is done in large quantities. While a $0.99 (paid) app may get 100 organic downloads in a day, a Freemium game using the pay per install model may get 2,500+ downloads in a day.

If your intention is to publish and monetize by selling ad space on your app, you will most likely be required to install an SDK (Software Developers Kit) into your app in order for them to work. However, if your goal is to purchase ad space through the pay-per-install method, it won't be necessary for you to install the SDK.

It's important to note that each SDK requires a certain amount of time to install into your app, but that can range anywhere from 30 minutes to two weeks. This varies because each app has its own set of code that requires integration. Also keep in mind that if you work with a 3rd party engine, such as the popular UNITY engine, it may add an additional layer of complexity, as you may have to create a custom wrapper to be able to integrate it.

It can difficult to gauge which MMP is right for you, as every app and circumstance is different. Each time you integrate one requires a resubmission to the app store. So determining the best fit can become a lengthy process. Choose what is best for your situation, keeping in mind that aside from offering the basic benefits of being able to monetize through publishing or promote your app by advertising across their network, there are some other benefits specific to each one and no two are the same. Below is a list of my top choices:

- Chartboost: A top choice for many publishers because of what they offer in terms of revenue generation using their automated system. They also offer free cross-promotion, and you can even do direct deals with other developers.

- Tapjoy: One of the biggest and most reputable MMP's. Developers like Zynga, Ngmoco and Glu mobile actively use them because of the high fill rates they offer. Aside from the usual services, they also offer developers a virtual goods/currency hosting service, real-time reporting and custom creative design services.

- Tapgage: Although they're the new kid on the block, they offer developers high fill rates and the highest value cross-promotional service out there. At a 4:5 ratio, with incredible professionalism and courtesy with the team, they really cater to the indie developer.

- Playhaven: An advertiser's best friend, they offer a low-cost solution with some of the lowest CPI rates. They also offer real-time analytics with stats for hourly, daily, weekly and monthly active users. If you're looking to run a strong burst campaign on a budget, these guys are the way to go. Their knowledgeable staff are super-friendly, too.

- Admob: Another heavy-hitter in the MMP space. They have built a reputation of offering developers some of the highest earnings for publishers, as well as offering cross-promotion and solid advice on advertising and marketing. Check out their guide to the app galaxy.

MMP Aggregates, which allow you to manage all your ad networks under a single unified system, have recently become available. With these systems, it only requires you to install one SDK to serve as a container that houses the other SDK's. This benefits the developer by allowing them to serve ads from all the major networks while giving them the ability to manage and prioritize each. Developers can make quicker determinations of which service works best for their app and manage them in real time. In my opinion, the top three are MoPub, Adexlink and Mobclix.

Chapter 3: Preparation For Marketing

The First Few Weeks

Prior to app launch, you'll need to make some preparations. Because when your app is approved, your marketing efforts need to be very aggressive during the first couple of weeks — and I mean a full-on sprint! You only have a small window of opportunity to capitalize and gain momentum.

During this time, you need a lot of downloads at once to gain rank in the App Store — and obtaining a high ranking in the App Store is of utmost importance, because that is what will drive organic downloads of your app. Make sure that in advance of your launch, you have a well-developed marketing plan.

This chapter deals with what you need to prepare in advance for the upcoming marketing campaign.

The Tools Of The Trade

Social Networks

It's best to set up your social networking accounts early, so starting these in parallel with the app is not an uncommon practice. The two social media networks you should be concerned with for a pre-launch campaign, (as of this writing) are a Facebook page and a Twitter account. During and after the development process you can use these to draw interest with posts about your development process, sharing concepts along the way to excite your growing fan base. After development and at the time of launch, you can use them as a marketing platform, encouraging your fans to help you re-share your posts among their friends to spread the word. Post-launch, you will use them to continue to communicate with your established fan base. Let them know about future updates, take polls and most importantly listen and engage them. People like it when you give a little personal attention to their concerns.

By setting these up early, you build up an audience to communicate with during the process, and a hopefully a substantial following by the time your app launches. I've seen many developers wait until the last minute to do this; on launch day, it does you no good if you have zero fans or followers to announce it to. Don't be "that" developer: start this part early. As for Twitter, Don't feel you have to post daily, or share random thoughts for the sake of having a post. Just set it up and start to follow some iOS-related Twitter accounts. Others will begin to find and follow you, growing your network. There are also a number of iOS reviewers and game journalists to be found through such social media, and it doesn't hurt to engage with them occasionally.

The iTunes App Store

The iTunes App Store is without a doubt the single most powerful agent of exposure for your iOS app/game. Visibility in the iTunes App Store is key. All other methods of marketing should be supportive of your main goal, which is achieving a high ranking within the App store.

You can achieve exposure within the app store in two ways: through being featured by Apple, and by gaining a high ranking for your category. While achieving high ranking is a bit more under your control. You can't buy your way into being featured, so it's more about luck than anything else. However, there are some things you can do to improve your chances.

Featured Apps

Developers who have been fortunate enough to have their apps featured by Apple in "New & Noteworthy," "Staff Favorites," or other featured categories know that the exposure received during those few weeks is priceless. Unfortunately, only a few receive that honor, and it is something that cannot be purchased. Matt Rix said of being featured in the App Store, "it's like winning a lottery, but a lottery where you work really really hard to buy your ticket." (Read more about the development of his game, Trainyard, here.)

Apple does not reveal their selection process. They don't favor any particular developer, nor can they be bribed or manipulated (not that I've tried!). They uphold a high standard of business ethics in attempt to keep selection fair for everyone. What this means is that, although you shouldn't count on being featured from Apple, it does happen. (You should also know that even apps that are chosen can fade back into obscurity once their time in the spotlight has passed.)

That said, here are 10 things to keep in mind if you want to improve your chances:

1. **Good Quality:** The design should be solid in form and function, with smooth, fluid mechanics. The aesthetics should be appealing to the general public, and the app should be free of bugs and errors. Overall, it should be a quality app.
2. **Useful/Fun:** If it's an application, it should offer something useful and of interest to consumers. If it's a game, it should be fun and engaging.
3. **Nice Presentation:** The icon, app store copy, and screenshots should be high-quality, well presented, and as error-free as possible.
4. **Unique:** Apple prefers to expose apps and games that offer something new. Clusters of similar apps or copycats rarely get featured, unless they offer something unique that sets them apart from the others.
5. **Utilize Apple's Proprietary Features:** By making use of the Accelerometer, the camera, maps, compass, or even the microphone, the app shows off Apple's built-in technology —and they like that.
6. **High ratings:** High ratings and good customer reviews are important. Typically they feature apps with three stars or higher. (If your app is new to the market with no ratings, this rule doesn't apply.)

7. **Media:** The media plays a role in being selected, if somewhat indirectly. Apple hand-picks which apps are featured, but first they have to know about the apps. If your app is featured on one of the main app coverage sites, like <u>Toucharcade</u> or <u>Appadvice</u>, then it's more likely that Apple will notice your app, and you stand a better chance at being included for evaluation.

8. **Seasonal:** Apple often features seasonal-themed apps and games during that season.

9. **Follow Apple's standards:** Apple has a set of art and design standards for developers called the IOS Human Interface Guidelines. Simple things, like utilizing swipes to navigate pages (as opposed to using buttons), help to keep the user experience more native to Apple's platforms. The more you adhere to their standards, the greater the chances of your app being featured.

10. **Design Awards:** There are several <u>app awards</u> out there, but the one that is most beneficial to your app getting featured is Apple's own <u>Apple Design Awards.</u> Just applying here will get you exposed to some of the top app critics inside Apple.

Rankings

Rankings play an important part in discovery and exposure for you app. In fact, the top method of gaining sustained organic exposure for your app is being visible in the App Store through a high rank. 80% of all sales are made via the App Store's ecosystem.

There are 124 countries in the app store, and each of them ranks your app independently. Over 80% of all our game downloads come from the U.S, so I'll be using the U.S. App Store as my primary point of reference on this subject.

The App Store will list the top 300 apps in any given category, but nothing beyond that. There are currently 22 individual categories for apps, one of which is games. The games category itself is made up of 20 individual sub-categories. This gives you a total of 41 categories with 100 rankings = 4,100 good spots of visibility.

If your app or game is not listed within this top 4,100, then it's practically invisible to the consumer. In fact, being visible in the App Store is your single greatest sales agent, so your your goal should be to achieve the highest ranking position possible for your chosen category.

No one knows for sure the exact formula that Apple uses to rank and list apps in the App store, but research points to these as the three primary factors:

1. Number of Downloads

2. High Ratings/Reviews
3. Frequency of User Engagement

When an app is listed in the top five for a given category, the user sees it immediately: no scrolling or finger movement is involved, therefore it is the position with the most visibility. To see the remaining top 25, the user must swipe his finger upward. To see the next 25, he must click on the "Twenty Five More" button at the bottom. This process is repeated over until he reaches the bottom (which is #300). Due to trust, time, and even laziness, people are less inclined to scroll far down the list to make a purchase. So the higher up you are on that list, the more exposure your app will have, and thus more downloads.

The competition is fierce as apps are playing a game of "king of the hill." This dynamic is so powerful and the advantage so huge that it has spawned off numbers businesses to drive discoverability, such as mobile marketing platforms. With these platforms, you will often pay over a $1.00 for each install of your free app and even more if it's a paid app.

While it would normally be considered a bad idea to pay people to take something for free, the app store economy works differently, in that the higher rankings means you are exposed to an even larger audience. This results in greater organic downloads.

Here are some stats gathered for each specific category for paid apps in the U.S Market. (The numbers on the left column indicate rank and the other columns tell how many downloads you need to achieve that ranking. They are not definitive because they fluctuate constantly and other factors play into ranking — so use it as a guide rather than a rule.)

Education	Entertainment	Finance	Music	Sports	Reference	
Rank #1 – 5	700+	1500+	200+	600+	300+	500+
Rank #6 – 25	N/A	725+	125+	N/A	150+	N/A
Rank #26 – 50	N/A	350+	N/A	N/A	N/A	N/A
Rank #51 – 75	N/A	150+	N/A	N/A	N/A	N/A
Rank #75 -100	N/A	75+	N/A	N/A	N/A	N/A

To get into the top 25 overall (Paid) apps in the U.S. App Store, you need around 3,500 downloads per day. Angry birds, recently hit 10 million paid downloads in the App Store and remains in the #1 spot for many countries.

Plan For Regular Updates

With each update, you are being re-introduced on the device as well as on websites like AppShopper. There are even apps, like Free App Finder, that call attention to updates, price drops, etc. You don't have to take any action for this to happen, as the apps and websites ping the app store (and various other sources) for the updated info. The takeaway here is that there are multiple places that cover updates offering you additional exposure inadvertently.

If the update is significant, it offers the opportunity for you to issue a press release, which will also help bring it into the public's attention. With every update you can:

- Make improvements to the game, add new features and bug fixes to keep your current fans happy and loyal.
- Get new ratings and reviews (with most cases)
- Re-categorize your product (if the category you have currently doesn't produce desired results or has grown stale)
- Inform the media, through press release(s), and get the word out

That said, updates should be part of your continued effort and marketing. Release a good game, but plan for future updates, even during the development of the game. The trick is to always leave room for more. Also consider that many ideas will flop, no matter how cool you think they are, because the consumer may want something different. As a digital product, you have the option to iterate on it, so take advantage of this. Listen to the community and get feedback after launch. Engage with the people to see what they like or dislike, and try to add the stuff they want to the next update. Not only will the fans appreciate it, you make a better experience for newcomers as well.

Pricing Strategy

Most apps are sold at just $0.99, the reason for this being volume. The cheaper it is, the more people buy it; the more sales it has, the higher it will rank in the app store. Higher ranking leads to more exposure, which leads to more organic sales, which further helps it sustain a high ranking. It is what sets apart the app store economy apart from other markets and is the reason why games that would normally be $50 in retail store sell for just $0.99 in the iTunes store. Free or very cheap games sell more in volume.

Because of this, most developers will price their apps low to remain competitive in this market.

Unless your app is based on the freemium or ad-supported models, I would avoid jumping to the lowest price point ($0.99) right away. If possible, I recommend you keep your pricing at what you truly value your app to be for at least the first 6 months. After that, do scheduled price drops over the next six months until you get to the low point. Here are some points to keep in mind:

- **Launch sale:** For the first 2 weeks, I suggest a launch sale. A few reasons for this are: 1) it encourages users to make a purchase before the price goes up, 2) any written reviews or articles published during this time will usually state the price, which will remain permanent on those websites and get more views, and 3) it will compound your marketing efforts. Since you will be doing a big marketing push at launch, the additional appeal of a launch sale will add to the benefit and make it that much more appealing.

- **Price drops:** Do regular price drops from time to time to spike your rankings for a couple days before setting the price back to normal. Timing them with your updates is a good strategy—if there are no updates, then every two months or so is also a good measure. Several of the top publishers, like EA and Gameloft, do price drops every Holiday. It is the perceived value of a "sale" that people tend to gravitate towards and because it's for a limited time, it's also a call to action. There is also the added benefit that several websites, twitter accounts and even other apps will monitor App Store price drops and spread the news for you, so you get some free marketing out of it as well.

- **Adjust your app store copy**: During a price drop, you will want to adjust your App Store copy so that the header will let any potential buyers know your app is on sale for a limited time. An example of this would be: "*** 36 HOUR SALE – 66% off ***" right at the top. This encourages users to make a purchase just from the opportunity alone.

An important thing to note is that once you've set your price at the minimum $0.99, you will lose the benefit of being able to do price drops. Dropping it to "free" for a limited time doesn't work with this method because putting the app into the "free" category has no effect on rankings in the paid category. So it's always better to start off a little higher so that you have some wiggle room for these things.

We initially set the price for *My Virtual Girlfriend* at $2.99. Once things stabilized after launch, it was averaging 30 downloads per day (at $2.99 = $100 gross). With a price drop, it would typically get 60 sales per day, which at $0.99 = $60 (gross). Although the sales doubled, the gross revenues were significantly less, but the benefit was that it would gain ranking in the app store exposing it to more people.

Marketing Services

Although this book is geared toward the indie developer who prefers to "market it themselves," there of course comes a time when we could all use a bit of support. I've found two resources that deserve a mention because of their reputation and flexibility.

Comboapp and Appular are two great services that cater every budget. They have proven themselves as reputable marketing companies that offer value for their services. I would recommend considering their services as "reinforcements" to what you can't or are not willing to do.

Your App Store Page

The app store page is a very important, yet often overlooked element. You should address this at just prior to submission to the app store. It is significant because it is essentially the last checkpoint before a potential customer downloads your app from the app store. Let's tackle these in order of importance:

1. **Icon:** As the first thing a potential buyer will see, your app's icon is very important, so don't underestimate its power. It should look professional, attractive, grab the attention, and should attempt to offer some indication as to what your app is about. This is your first chance to attract a customer, so don't miss out on it. The artist in me has this advice to offer you:

   - First concept the icon out as a 57 x 57 pixel thumbnail. You need to make sure it reads well at that size, because that is how it's most often viewed.
   - Once you are comfortable, create the high detail version (512 x 512), which you will resize to fit the other sizes you need.
   - View the image at it's smaller sizes to see how well it holds up 29 x 29, 57 x 57, 58 x 58, and 114 x 114 pixels.

2. **App Name:** Along with your icon, this is one of the first things a potential customer will see. App names are important because they play a very important part in App store SEO (Search Engine Optimization, or the process of optimizing the text on websites in order to rank higher in search engines). The search engines send out "crawlers" that scan through the text on your site and identify "key words" associated with your site. When a user goes to a search engine and types in a word, the search engine must rank and display the results, which are based on the SEO of your site, including the App name, your business name, keywords you enter in at submission and words found on your page.

   Being that each word in your app name is essentially a primary keyword associated with your app, your app's title should be simple, yet descriptive text. Having a name that has to do with what you think people will search for is key. If you are to make a fighting game with monsters, "Fighting Monsters" might be a good choice. It might not be the most creative choice, but it's to the point and it is certain to rank high for those searching for a fighting game involving monsters.

3. **Screenshots:** Your app's first screenshot is the third item on the list of things a potential customer is likely to see. Most of the time, the user will bypass the descriptive text in order to see a screenshot (as we are visual creatures). So make sure to select a screenshot that shows your app in all its glory. Since you have five slots to show, fill them up. Keep them varied to show all the flavors. I usually take anywhere from 25–50 or so screenshots, then pick my top 5 from that.

4. **Header:** This is the first two lines of your app store description. It should be catchy and invite the user to investigate further as the complete description of your app is not shown by default. Visitors must click on the "more" link to expand the remainder of the description. If this is your app's first submission, then the best use of this space is simply to state what the game is about. After the app gains some exposure, you can use it to display various quotes by critics or any media coverage it has received.

5. **Full Description:** After the header comes the rest of the description, allowing the viewer to read further into what you are offering. You may want a couple sentences that elaborate on the header, or you could describe it through a small 4–6 sentence story. Try to avoid using adjectives like "fun" and "addictive" — this may seem like a good way to build excitement for your viewing audience, but it's actually unnecessary fluff. Better to use the space on SEO keywords that can actually improve your ranking in searches.

If your game is already in the App Store and has already gained news coverage or reviews, consider quoting some of the more favorable lines from the review, to add validation that the app is worth purchasing, either in the header or at the top of the description. Use the body of the description to describe your game and be sure to include a bulleted list. At the end of the description, leave a link to the video trailer and or website so people can get more info.

Also note that your App Store page is cloned into a web page and as an App Store preview page. The preview page is indexed by search engines such as Google and Yahoo, and has actually outperformed the official websites in many cases due to their web-friendly SEO. More information on App Store copy and SEO is available in this Article: App Store SEO: The Impact of iTunes web preview by Weldon Dodd.

It's important to strike a balance between simplicity and hype on your app store page. Using an excessive amount of adjectives to glorify your app will appear as over-hyped and may even disenchant some viewers as it becomes difficult for the users to navigate to the information they really want to know. But keeping this overly simple may also have a negative effect. It can underwhelm the user, giving the impression that nothing exciting is going on.

When you do use adjectives to describe elements about your app, use them sparingly so they hold more potency. Refrain from using the generic adjectives like "fun," "polished," and "unique," as Eli Hodapp, the Editor-in-Chief at <u>toucharacde.com</u> mentions in his article <u>here</u>.

Press Releases

The goal of a press release is to get the news of your release to a media channel with the hopes that they will publish something about it. Whether it's web, TV, radio, podcast, or print, each offer the chance to expose your product to their viewers. Most of the major media exposure that *My Virtual Girlfriend* has received was a direct result from a press release.

I believe that a well-crafted press release is one of the most significant marketing efforts you can make. Services such as prMac and gamespress both offer creation and distribution services of a press release. I recommend you use at least two or more for distribution, ideally one that targets the mobile apps industry and one that targets the video game industry.

Creating a Press Release

You can opt to have one drafted up, or you can write it yourself. If you decide to tackle this on your own, keep in mind that you must write them for an entirely a new audience: you are writing it for journalists, and editors within the media, not the general public.

The media has a their own set of standards when it comes to press releases. There is a specific format you should follow, and spelling and grammar are crucial. Distribution services know this well and will reject your submission if it fails to meet these standards, so be sure to double-check everything before submitting. I've paid for people to write a press release and I've also created them myself: the bonus material in this book contains a sample of a press release I've done. You can use it as a template to get you started.

As an added precaution, I usually have a friend of mine, Deborah Fike, look over my submissions before I send them out. She is both a writer and a producer in the games industry, and knows these two things very well. She is available for freelance work and writing services.

Because journalists in the media often choose what topics they wish to cover, it's necessary for them to have an interest in your subject matter. A few things can play into this and motivate them to write about your app:

- They think it's of interest to their viewers. Topics that are specific to their media channel jump to the front of the line.

- It's of personal interest to them, or something they like to cover—this is especially true on smaller websites and blogs.
- Trending or controversial matter, If you offer something that may strike them as having to do with current affairs or it's controversial in some way.

The Headline

The media are bombarded with hundreds of press release submissions per week, so they often just skim through the headlines to see which ones might be of interest for them to cover. That being the case, the first step is to grab their attention with a great headline. A number of things contribute to a good headline, which you can find listed in greater detail in this article by Mickie Kennedy: How to Write Better Press Release Headlines.

When To Send Them Out

Press releases propagate information across multiple websites, RSS feeds, bloggers and other news media. Every time I've put out a press release, I've had major coverage on my game: including late night talk show with Comedian George Lopez of "Lopez Tonight!", Discover, Gamepro, Nettavisen, and MSNBC (which was reposted on Kotaku). While not all press is positive, it is still exposure. It gains notoriety, and people are curious to see what others are talking about. Needless to say, sale spikes occur every time a major media player covers your app.

These releases should be sent out at two crucial periods: at launch, and with every significant update. This is why I plan a press release with every update because in addition to improving the game experience, it allows me to have some "news" to share with the media and the fans alike. For any press release you must prepare the following:

- A well crafted and attention getting press release (if you pay for it, it will generally run you from $150-250), or you can do it yourself.
- Screenshots
- Official trailer or game play video
- An official game website
- An official Business website
- Money, Plan to spend about $300 on each press release (creation and distribution)

An often overlooked, and most critical component to getting a press release noticed, is to get the positive attention of the journalist you are sending it to. An interesting article titled: "How to annoy a games journalist with a press release," includes contributions from several reputable journalists explaining some of their biggest pet peeves when receiving a press release. I've summarized the top five things you should be aware of:

1. **Be sincere and be personable.** Journalists will know when you're fabricating stories. They just want to hear the truth, and appreciate a bit of personal touch as well. They realize you may be blasting this out to hundreds of other journalists, but for your part you should at least create a top 10 list that you both email and approach in a more personal way.

2. **Don't fluff, boast or brag.** (This ties into #1, Sincerity) Avoid telling them how great your game is or using buzzwords and sounding overconfident.

3. **Get to the content and explain the "why."** Explain what is newsworthy and why.

4. **Don't annoy or be pushy with Expectations or frequent follow-up.** Allow them time to digest it and even then, don't have expectations that they will write. Remember that it is their choice to write, and being pushy only serves to annoy them and blacklist your company.

5. **Be targeted.** Target the right journalists. Don't write to "moms with apps" if your game is possibly the most bloody game in iTunes.

Celebrity Endorsements

Words With Friends developers got their big break when musician John Mayer tweeted "Words With Friends is the new Twitter." Shortly thereafter, they experienced a significant spike in sales that propelled them to the high rankings in the app store, combined with the virility of a social game. There are currently over 6.5 million downloads of the game. Similarly, *My Virtual Girlfriend* received a significant amount of downloads after actor and comedian George Lopez joked about it during the opening monologue of his late night TV show, Lopez Tonight!.

If a celebrity chooses to speak about your product, it can be very good for sales. However, one should not count on celebrity endorsements to occur as part of their marketing strategy. It is completely by chance that this would naturally occur, and I don't recommend paying for an endorsement (as it would be likely you would not recoup the costs). However, if you do have that chance, take full advantage of it in any way you can to further amplify its effect. Spread it through your social networks, mention it on the app's website, in the app store copy, in any advertisement banners and any other ways that continue to push the momentum.

Chapter 4: Post-Launch

App Reviews

Probably the most popular approach for developers to obtain exposure for their apps is by having their apps reviewed on app-related sites. In many cases getting reviewed is free, but for the sites that do offer them for free, those coveted spots can often be quite difficult to obtain.

Popular review sites such as Touch Arcade, Slide to Play and 148 apps are so swamped with review requests that it is unlikely they will even write you back to confirm they received your submission. (I've found this to be the case about 90% of the time.) These sites focus on what's popular and trending already. The ones that do write back will confirm your submission, but that's about it. If you try to establish an email dialog with them it will likely work against you, as you end up just pestering them.

And don't try to buy your way into a review: that won't work either. They will simply refer you to their ad sales department for purchasing an advertisement on their site. These sites have built a reputation around unbiased app reviews and they make it a point not to take compensation for one. While this is good for the industry as a whole, it kinda sucks for the little developers who can't afford ad space on those sites, (which don't offer a great ROI anyway) and you have smaller odds of receiving a review from them organically, due to the amount of submissions they receive.

So if you have no traction in the App store, the odds are not in your favor. However, they do seek out the unknown gems of the App store, so if you have an exceptional app that pushes above mediocrity, there is a chance you might get a review. If it's a truly unique and engaging experience, it further increases your chances of receiving some well-deserved coverage on it. I've listed below the top five most popular app review sites:

1. Toucharcade
2. Slide to Play
3. 148 Apps
4. App Advice
5. App Safari

Requesting reviews from less popular sites can evoke a response back, but they usually do so in one of two ways:

1. They will state that they received your submission and added it to their review queue, but don't know when they will get around to the review. In the meantime you should buy ad space on their site to gain exposure for your app. So instead of you getting a review, you get solicited back for costly ($$$) ad space on their site.

    If they respond back this way, it is usually just to dangle a carrot in front of you to get you to buy an ad; they don't actually intend to write a review of your app. Ask them explicitly if it will guarantee a review within a certain amount of time to avert being played for a fool. If they make no offer or promises in this regard, it's probably best to decline the ad space offer, as most ad spaces on small sites don't offer a good ROI.

2. They write you back to confirm your submission and let you know your app has been added to their queue to be reviewed. However, if you pay for an "expedited" review, it will happen a within a short period of time. At first glance this may appear just as shady as an ad offer, since they usually cost around the same price. However, paying for a review is much better than paying for an ad, and here's why:

    ○ Ads are only temporary, they go away after the duration of the campaign.
    ○ Reviews can leave a permanent backlink to your app's website, granting your site better search engine results.
    ○ You can use the ratings and quotes from them for marketing purposes.
    ○ You can propagate the review through all your social networks.
    ○ If it's a video review, you can use this link to the video for marketing purposes.

Although these sites may charge for a review, many of them value their reputation as much as the popular sites do and are aspiring to grow. Several of them have pledged to remain unbiased during the review process and they disclaim up front that you are not paying for the result, only that results happens quicker.

Sites such as Appcraver offer this type of service. The fact is, this isn't such a bad deal. If you're not already in the Top 100 in the App Store, they probably wouldn't have reviewed your game anyway. So getting exposure on some of the less popular sites can really be worth the cost. (Unfortunately, my personal experience with App Craver is that they were about 15 days late delivering on their promise, but they did eventually deliver.) It's pretty clear to see that the result was unbiased. See for yourself, and read it here: Romance Your iPhone with My Virtual Girlfriend.

It takes some time to contact reviewers manually. You should do this as soon as your game is available, but after your press release. It can be frustrating emailing them one by one, but be patient and professional, or you could end up in a sticky situation, like this guy. So for most indie developers, their best bet is a smaller app review site, blogger or a YouTube video reviewer. You may still have to pay for an "expedited" review, and/or for ad space, but at least it's affordable and you will get a review.

Below, I've listed some of the sites that I recommend for the indie developer who has a small budget to work with. I've used all of these and found them to have exceptional value and the best return on investment.

- Appdictions - Offers a nice variety of promotions at affordable prices.
- Crazy Mikes apps - Offers entertaining and often humorous video reviews
- iPhoneGlance - Very friendly staff and inexpensive reviews
- Cool iPhone and iPad apps - Offers affordable reviews then promotes them heavily.
- iViewApps - Offers affordable reviews and advertisements
- iFanzine.com - An iPhone game fan site that offers candid reviews as well as ads.
- Alphadigits.com - An iPhone and Android review site, they offer reviews, articles and promotion of apps.

The above list is just some of my top picks for inexpensive coverage for your app. The bonus material included in this book has a more comprehensive list that offers all the major and minor app review sites, bloggers, YouTube-ers, and more. It is a spreadsheet template that lists several websites and is set up so that you can track your progress with those sites.

Articles

An alternative to an app review is a standard web article. The main difference between an article and a review is that in an article they don't offer a rating for the app, and it's generally less opinionated throughout. Writers and bloggers tend to write "articles," whereas reviewers will write "reviews." Articles tend to focus on what the app does, and typically leave the opinion up to the viewer to decide for themselves.

Articles range in size from a simple paragraph on a blog to elaborate video demonstrations. The author usually posts links to the app, and you can also ask them to link back to your website for more information. Any inbound links to the app's website help out with its ranking in search engines.

And although articles tend to get less traffic than that of a review site, having an article written about your app/game is still very beneficial. You will gain insight regarding your audience and can use the feedback on future iterations of your app. Whatever the case for your piece, always follow up and answer any questions or comments that usually occur below the post.

If you created an app that was not intended to be a big fuss, such as a simple utility app, or you think what you offer is lacking and you feel may receive a damaging review, an article may be the best way for your app to gain some exposure without killing your chances of a sale. You still gain the exposure for your app through their website or blog, and it offers their audience some insight about your product.

App Store Ratings And Written Reviews

Once your app is available in iTunes, user ratings and written reviews will become available for all to see. It's important to have a few ratings in there as soon as possible, as they will serve as a testament to others who read them. An app with no ratings is deemed as untrustworthy and becomes a hard sell. So it's crucial that you get something in there before people see that there are no ratings and pass on it. Friends and family (with iOS devices) are the best resource to get some reviews in quickly.

I usually hit up friends or family first via my personal Facebook account, letting them know that the app is now available in iTunes and asking them if they could to take a moment to download, rate, and write something about it in the iTunes app store and share my links on the social networks. The next set of people I ask are other iOS developers. You can do it in exchange for reviewing their app. If it's a paid app, I will usually just "gift" it to them through iTunes so I can save my promo codes for the app reviewers. There are more review sites than you will have promo codes for, so it's likely you will eventually run out long before contacting them all. Also note that reviewers will NOT purchase your game, so you need to make it easy for them.

The idea of having people you know rate and rank your game may seem like you're tipping the scales to your favor. This may or may not be the case, depending on how you go about this, but consider that either way, other player reviews will quickly start pouring in and work themselves into the average of the 5-10 people you could probably get to give you a rating. I should also mention that this is not an uncommon practice. Trust me when I say that nearly all developers solicit reviews from their own resources, from big companies to the smaller indie studios—they are just very discreet about it.

Now, that doesn't mean you should solicit everyone you know for 5 star reviews and ask them to write only good things about your app. On the contrary, I think there are ways to do this with integrity and still meet the objective. Have your friends and family offer a "fair" rating and review. Give them the option that if they can't find anything positive to say about your app, you would prefer they don't leave any feedback at all. Instead, have them email you their feedback. This way, you still get their feedback, which helps you to make future improvements, while not putting your faults on public display.

It's also best to steer clear of having friends and family write over-hyped, insincere or false reviews. You don't want a bunch of 5-star ratings that all making obvious false statements about your app. Most people will see right through this and you may even receive a backlash of angry players who were "tricked" into thinking it was something fantastic when it wasn't. They will go out of their way write a negative review and call you out as being fake or a ripoff. This is more damaging than the single sale you would get from it as it can hurt your credibility as a developer.

Forums

There are a few good iOS app-related forums out there you should be posting on to get the word out:

1. Toucharcade
2. Slidetoplay
3. iphoneworld.ca

You should post to forums at launch, and during any promotion or update you may offer. I've seen a fair amount of traffic to my website after making a post, then a trickle of traffic thereafter. A word of caution though: forums HATE spam and trolls, which in many cases this also includes developers just trying to get the word out. To avoid being banned, read the rules and post in the appropriate category. They usually set a specific place aside for developers to make app announcements. In most cases they want you to use only one thread per app. So if you post an update about your game three months down the road, continue from the previous post you created. Respect their rules or risked being ostracized from the community.

A forum post should include:

- A catchy headline for the title
- An introduction for the body of the message
- A simple description
- Product information: price, which devices it's for, age rating, etc.
- Features of the game, (bulleted list)
- Screenshots, and/or video
- Links to the app in iTunes (both paid and free versions)
- Links to the official website
- A closing statement (thank you note)

- Your signature (including your name, title, company name and email)

Be sure to follow-up after your post. Visit the site half a day or a day later to view comments and engage with the community. People appreciate real developers engaging with them and not just "hit-n-run'ers" (people that post something, then leave, never to be seen again). It can be a bit daunting to track and maintain forums posts so i suggest creating a bookmark in your browser, then spend some time dedicated to going through them on occasion.

<u>Facebook</u> is the standard for social media: it currently has over <u>800 million</u> users and spans nearly all the countries in the world. Here are some ways you can utilize Facebook for your social marketing efforts…

- **Fan Pages:** Set up a Facebook fan page for your game. A fan page offers you a forum to share information, screenshots, announcements, and the ability to engage with the community. A big benefit to this is that when you post something, it will appear on your fan's pages and it also gives them the option to share your message with their friends. Another benefit is the "like" button, which helps to validate to others that the game is popular. In addition to this, every time you post an update through the fan page, it posts to the wall of the user who liked it.

I ask fans of our games to repost the posts to their walls so they can share with their friends, which is a great catalyst for viral marketing. The fan page may also serve as the primary social hub for anyone that enjoys your game as an alternative to setting up an isolated website forum.

- **Other page posts:** I've had some limited success with posting to other iOS, related fan page walls, in effort to obtain new fans for my games. Any time you have an announcement, you can post it to various iOS-related fan page walls. For whoever "likes" or is a fan of that page, it will re-distribute that message to that user's wall. So if you find a Facebook fan page that has 1500 fans you can potentially post to all their walls at once. I can see the excitement in your eyes, but don't get all post crazy just yet. People can mark posts as spam and you can be penalized by Facebook if you do too much, too often.

- **Friends:** Let your friends know! Ask for their support! If they are a true friends, they will understand and help support your efforts with a re-post, or at least a "like" or comment.

<u>Twitter</u> Set up your Twitter account early on in the development of your game. Don't wait until after your game is developed to do this. It takes time to grow a following—it took me

nearly eight months to grow to 2,000 fans on my Twitter account. Sure, there are programs you can purchase that will get you a bunch of followers, but most of those followers are just false accounts: bots and other non-personal accounts that are there for the sole purpose of acquiring new followers for their own agenda. You don't want to waste your time there; grow your Twitter account organically through time, and interaction.

Also, to be quite frank, I've seen little return on investment just announcing things to my followers on Twitter. If I'm lucky, I'll get less than a handful of people that will visit the link in the announcement that I offer. I've lost more followers by spamming my Twitter with announcements that I've gained from it—I've come to find out that's NOT the way to market yourself on Twitter. What I've learned from some social media experts is that the better way to use Twitter is to establish real relationships with people who are genuinely interested in what you're offering, organically and over time. Engage with people regularly, but don't push them to anything, it's futile. Once your game is released you can also use the Search box to find out who's discussing it and engage with them. This is a much more productive method than using it solely to get the word out, as it takes up too much time and the rewards are just not there.

Video Hosting Sites. Sites such as Youtube and Vimeo are great for both hosting a video and gaining additional exposure. These sites allow you to upload and store videos for free. You should include a link to the video where appropriate, such as in user forums and press releases, and be sure to embed them in your website as well. One of the benefits to using these services over hosting on your own site is that you don't pay for bandwidth, since the data is being pulled from the host site. You also gain organic exposure for your app.

People have found these sites as a great resource for entertainment and information. Over time, it helps you to acquire new users who are interested in what you have to offer. So when you create your trailer or demo, be sure to upload to several video hosting sites so that you can maximize your chances of gaining exposure. My top choices are YouTube, Vimeo and Dailymotion but I've included a larger list toward the end of the ebook.

Paid social media traffic. You can acquire fans for your Facebook page very inexpensively through services available on sites like Fiverr.com. While most of the users may not have genuine interest in your product, some will be curious and investigate. The bigger benefit is having a few thousand fans as opposed to a few hundred because it's comforting for people to belong to part of a larger group than a smaller one.

All offers are priced at just $5, and there are several varieties to take advantage of. In fact the voice-overs for the level 20 screen in our game, *My Virtual Girlfriend*, were purchased from an offer by a similar type of website. If Fiverr isn't for you, several spin-off sites have popped up since its inception (14+ Sites Like Fiverr).

Free Social Media Traffic. Many of the same people that sell Twitter fans, Facebook page likes and YouTube view packages on these sites, acquire these users from "Trade for Trade" types of social media sites. These sites are springing up all over now, and they are great for acquiring new fans, followers and viewers if you have the time to invest. These sites are basically free traffic trading social utilities that require you to sign up, provide your various social network accounts, and then offer you credits based on the number of people who like, follow, or view your sites. You earn these credits by either Liking, following or viewing others' sites, or you can purchase credits directly from the site. Here is a small list of a few sites that I've found that do this:

- Twiends
- Social Clump
- Let Us Follow
- Social Boosting
- Ad Socials
- Traffup
- You Like Hits

Social Media Share Tools

Social media tools, such as <u>Stumbleupon</u>, <u>Digg</u>, and <u>Reddit</u>, all allow you and others to redistribute news. Most blog and review sites provide a convenient way for you to share any of their articles with a simple click of the button. These are known as "social media share tools" and "social media bookmarks." Make sure to set up accounts with at least the top three, if not the top 10 before you launch your game, because when a site does end up doing some coverage on your app, you want to help re-distribute that information across the web. And you don't want to be fumbling around, trying to set up accounts while trying to redistribute information.

News loses momentum and is not considered "new" if you're trying to share it a week later. Since there are several of these sites that re-distribute information, it's best to set it all up early so that you're prepared at launch to re-distribute the news quickly. Make sure to have the "<u>add this</u>" suite of social sharing buttons on your website, allowing others to share your game easily. I also installed the <u>"add this" toolbar for Firefox</u>, which allows me to share any articles I see done on my game by simply clicking a link on my toolbar, even if the blog doesn't have that specific sharing tool. Since we've already covered Facebook and Twitter, here is an ordered list of what I consider to be the remaining top three most relevant share tools for iOS developers (results may vary):

1. <u>Stumbleupon.com</u>
2. <u>Digg.com</u>
3. <u>Reddit.com</u>

Note: Although <u>Linkedin</u> can be a good tool to make an occasional announcement in your status update, it's generally frowned on by industry peers if you spam the professional community with self-interests. My suggestion is to limit yourself to only original announcements (and occasionally significant updates) to your status message. Avoid bulk messaging, direct and group posts (unless it's appropriate for that forum/group). Also, I would encourage you to provide links to your games website and your company's website, but only in your signatures and on your bio. It shows you're being professional and gives people a point of reference to investigate if they are curious.

App Promotional Service Apps

There are a number of apps that are dedicated to promoting other apps. They spread the news about free apps, price drops and incentives that might appeal to those looking for a bargain.

Freeappaday by ICS mobile is probably the most well-known of the bunch, due to their popularity and install base of over 4 million users. They use a unique approach to app promotion by taking what would normally be a paid app, making it free, and then notifying their users to come and download it. Since most people love to receive something of value for nothing, it attracts these digital bargain hunters like Apple fans to a new iPhone model announcement.

They do this by seeking out popular apps (i.e. those requested by fans), getting in touch with the developer (if the developer hasn't gotten in touch with them), and negotiating a contract where the developer agrees to make their app available for free for a short period of time, usually from one to five days. The promotional service company will promote the app during this period for a fee, revenue sharing for a duration of time, or both.

At first glance this may seem ludicrous — paying for a company to offer your game up for free to an audience of millions, where is the logic in that? But it's a numbers game. The concept is that the app becomes available for free on the promotion date. The promotion company puts your app in the spotlight by making it their "featured free app" and notifying their multitude of users that this new game that used to cost $X.99 is now free, and encourages users to come and download it. They do this across their website and in the app itself. A mass of users will download and play the free app during the promotion and over the next few days, a certain percentage of them will spread the word virally about your game with their friends. Once the promotion has ended and your app's price goes back to normal, the word of mouth has caught the interest of extended friends and people, thus driving regular purchases as the price is now back to normal.

Promotional companies have experienced a great deal of success using this model. I can testify that it does in fact work as intended. I tried this with *My Virtual Girlfriend* in January of 2011 with FreeAppADay. Just two weeks before the promotion, the app was getting about 30 downloads per day at $0.99. Then Christmas and that video with George Lopez hit and downloads and rankings both went up, just one week before the scheduled promotion. Since the game broke the Top 100 and was currently ranked at #60 in paid entertainment apps, it finally got some traction and I was feeling very uneasy about rocking the boat with the promotion. After all, taking it from a $0.99 app to free meant I would lose my current ranking for that category because free apps have their own ranking system.

During our promotion, which lasted a single day, *My Virtual Girlfriend* received over 50,000 downloads. But despite the positive numbers, the day was still full of stress for me: I had just achieved a decent rank in the App store (something I'd been trying at for a year), and now my app would be de-listed out of the paid category! It was too late to turn back, having already signed a contract, so I simply stayed in close contact with ICS mobile. They assured me it was going to be okay, and indeed when it was over and my app went back to the paid category, I saw it climb the charts all the way to the top 33 position for paid entertainment apps. The falloff from this promotion lasted only a few weeks before it went back to normal sales, but in the end we both came out a little ahead for that month.

The best candidates for this type of service are under-exposed, good quality, paid games. The fees associated with these services can be quite pricey depending on the service, and it requires a significant amount of installs in order to serve well. So before committing to running a campaign with one of these services, do a gut check and ask yourself if your game is something that has the potential to appeal to a mass audience. If not, this may not be the best route to go. There are several of these app promotional service apps out there that use the method above, and some even have their own unique spin, such as:

- FreeAppaDay (Link to their app in the iTunes app store)
- Freeappreport (Link to their app in the iTunes app store)
- MonsterFreeApps (Link to their app in the iTunes app store)

Internal Cross-Promotion

This is one of the most effective methods for app discovery. If you're an app developer, you have more than one app, and you are not doing this, do it. Now. You can use internal cross-promotion to drive installs for your current apps, and for any future apps you develop. All you need is a system in place that allows for this to happen. Fortunately, many of the mobile monetization platforms already provide these systems and even offer them free to developers, all it requires is the installation of their SDK.

You can use their system, or you can opt to build your own. If you choose this option, I suggest you don't just create a method of directly promoting your other apps, but one that allows you to layer in other systems on top, including your own. This give you multiple options. Here are a few points in favor of each…

Using their system:

- Little code time — just integrate their SDK.
- They offer other services, such as monetization and analytics.
- No maintenance (they do all the work and refining of the system).
- No direct fees! (although they may take a cut of your revenues from what you earn from using their system)

Creating your own system:

- Freedom of choice — you're not locked into a particular system.
- Do direct deals with other developers who may not use a particular system.
- Ability to shut on/off and weight different systems on the fly, without having to resubmit to Apple.

In my case, we opted to create our own system. Ours allows us to layer in other Mobile Monetization Platform SDK's on top of it, as well as having the option to run our own ads in it. It gives us the most flexibility and we are not locked into a particular system. Either choice is fine, it's just a matter of preference.

Chapter 5: Marketing

Your Budget

I typically set aside a budget of 10% of the previous month's revenues on marketing for the next month. On months where I'm about to push out an update out, or an entirely new app, I will raise up the budget to 15-20%. Web ads make up about 20% of that, paid reviews make up another 50%, and 20% in various other promotions.

Web and Banner Ads

Web ads are a subject of great debate among many iOS developers, as many developers find that ads don't translate well to direct sales of their apps. I find this to be true about 90% of the time, and even the other 10% is hard to measure. There is currently no way to track direct installs from a web ad, so all you can really do is measure click-through's and impressions to assess their value.

The ones that do seem to offer a good return on investment are difficult to find. This is also a moving target as new sites are popping up all the time, offering introductory prices on ad space and work hard to promote their site to gain additional footing. Others who are more established in their prices because their supplies of advertisers are met are just trying to turn a higher profit.

Don't count banner ads out entirely though—there are some good finds out there, as well as some indirect benefits associated with them you may not be aware of:

- **Increased product awareness**: Having ads with your logo or app icon placed on various websites increases your product awareness. Think of the time you may have seen an ad for a movie displayed on a billboard. At first glance you probably don't care. But then you see it also in a magazine, and then on TV or even a Taco bell cup. The more places it is seen, the more it demands your attention and sparks your curiosity, so there is a greater likelihood that you will investigate further. I find this especially beneficial when I'm doing a major promotional push, and will supplement with ad space on various sites as well.
- **It can get your foot in the door**: Sometimes an ad can establish the communication you need to get the attention of a review site. It may serve as a foot in the door that opens up a dialog if the site manager is being completely unresponsive when you solicited them for a review. Not to say that it will grant you a good review, or even a review at all, but just

that if you're having trouble reaching people on the inside, this can help in some instances.

- **Convenience:** If I find a website where I feel my ads are bringing in a reasonable return on investment, I'll keep it running on that site. It's an automated process that requires very little effort from my part: just a check-in once every couple of weeks to see that the numbers are staying steady. Since the sites offer some statistics on click-throughs it's easy for me to see what's working and what's not.

Do note that these methods are only used as supplemental support to my primary marketing efforts. I normally have about four websites that I advertise on regularly. When I'm about to do a big push in marketing, such as we do after a major update for one of our apps, I will ramp that up and advertise across eight or so app-related web sites for that month.

One of the better resources I use to find good information and to purchase web ads is BuySellAds, which allows you to track stats, and even A/B test. A few others include advertising space and isocket. You must maintain an advertising effort, and be reactive to anything that is showing diminishing returns. If an ad were to bring in more than the cost of it, then it would be a plus. However, there is no way to get true install stats from an ad. You can only measure how many "clicks" the ad has received. So I measure by this formula:

If the ad produces 5X the amount of click-throughs than the cost, it's a keeper. Example: If the ad is $50.00 per month and the site brings in 250 clicks per month, that is the minimum requirement for me to keep that ad running. Why 5X? Because a large percentage of those do not actually commit to buy after clicking. This is just a guess, but I would say probably 50-75% are just clicking to see more information about the product and don't actually make a purchase. So my 5X rule compensates for that.

I regularly advertise on appstoreapps.com, ipfun.org, and Mbtheme.com, as they've given me back good, consistent results month after month.

These may or may not perform well for you. Every app that is created has a unique target audience and thus its own advertising requirements. Therefore, keep these things mind when hunting for the right ad space:

- Find a site with an audience that is relevant to your app's target audience. iOS app and game sites are a good starting point, but finding ones that reach out to the same age and the right gender are what you should be focusing on. Think of your target demographic when considering ad placement.

- Find a space where your app can stand out. Some websites are so flooded with advertisements for apps it looks like Apple threw up the entire app store on that website. These sites may boast a high amount of traffic, but a crowded space full of other ads lessens the chance they will look at yours. Look for sites where it's not too crowded with banner ads and other graphic distractions.

Ad Placements And Alerts

Whether you're advertising your own apps, or someone else's product, it all falls within the "ad" realm. When and where these ads occur in your game has a lot to do with how effective you think the ad can be at that point and place. This is known as "Ad Placement," and is used to describe when and where the ad occurs within the app. There are several types of ad placement: some can be quite simple and passive, and others annoying and aggressive. Which methods you choose to employ will depend on several factors, but the primary consideration should be the app itself. If it is a paid app, (one that a user has to pay to obtain) it may be best to limit yourself to simply a "more apps" button, which still offers your users something without being intrusive.

However, If the sole purpose of your app is to offer discounts or freebies on a timed basis, then a push notification may be a great way of alerting your users to an offer they may want to know about before the time expires. I've listed the more common ad placements below, in order of most to least intrusive.

- **Push notifications:** Also known as "announcements", Although considered to be a very effective method of getting the user's attention, misuse by developers has given push notifications a bad rap; but in the right context, these notifications can be a great aid and marketing tool. Push notifications are a way to remotely message any user who has installed their app, much in the same way a user will be notified that they have a text message. They can occur at any time the developer wants them to, even when the phone is idle and no app is running.

  However, keep in mind that push notifications can only happen if the user has them enabled, and that the developer must offer the user the option to allow them to occur, (which happens during installation). Because push notifications are limited to a simple text dialog display, they do not allow for graphics or other creative eye candy (other than a small version of the app's icon.) A word of caution before going overboard with this method: it is regarded as the least desirable method for mobile advertising. Similar to how we regard email spam or perhaps the mobile device equivalent of a telemarketer calling your home. You can use them but use them wisely. You may risk getting in hot water with Apple and/or damaging your reputation.

- **Alerts:** Similar to push notifications, in that they display a text message, but a little more friendly. They are automated messages that occur at certain time triggers you specify. An example of an alert is when you haven't played with the app in 3 days and it reminds you with the alert, which displays a text message like: "You haven't played *My Virtual Girlfriend* in 3 days—she misses you!" Well, you get the point. It's a nice little reminder that can help with user retention.

- **Burst Ads:** These tend to surprise the user with a pop-up advertisement window. They usually occur at game launch, over the main menu or before the actual game-play session begins. These are less obnoxious than a push notification, as the player can dismiss the ad with a "close" button, but are still considered to be an aggressive form of advertising. Since they prompt the user to take action then and there, they can be an effective tool used to drive installations to an app.

- **Banner Ads:** These are prominently displayed in a specific area on the screen during the app/game session. If you are intending to use them, you should consider where they will appear on the screen, so as not to interfere with your existing UI. It's best to think about this during the design phase of your game. iAds and admob are some of the more commonly used ad networks and offer easy integration into your app. Many developers offer free apps and use banner ads to generate revenues. There have been a few case studies where this has proven to be quite an effective method of generating revenue in the earlier years of iOS, but what I'm hearing from most developers now is that they are not that great. As with most things iOS, what will really determine the if the revenues are significant or not is the quantity of downloads.

- **Interstitial Ads:** These ads generally take up a good portion of the page, if not the full page. They can be static images, animated or even videos being streamed from a server. They usually occur during game-play, but often in non-intrusive ways, such as in place of load screens, in-between levels, or at the end of the game. In any case, the occurrence of the ad is intermittent and placed well as not to dilute the game experience. Most have a timed dismissal button that will appear after a short duration, ensuring the user views at least a portion of the ad before it goes away.

- **More Button:** The simplest and least intrusive of app advertising is a more button. Every developer should be using this. These are usually a single button located on the main screen that when clicked on, displays a list of other apps. This can be the developers own apps, a friends apps, or even an offer wall from a mobile game monetization platform.

Chapter 6: Research & Resources

Essential Materials

I've provided several resources and links throughout the document, but I also wanted to offer up some great resources that are not directly covered, but offer exceptional value.

Google Products: Google is constantly innovating on existing ideas and adding new products. Not only do they have an awesome search engine, but they also have some really great tools that are useful for developers: all you need is a Google account. Signing up for a Gmail account will get you started and give you the means to gain access to a host of useful tools.

- Google Docs: The web equivalent of Microsoft office, it's online and accessible via your web browser. Access offers the ability to create documents, presentations, spreadsheets, forms, and flow charts. In fact, this very ebook was created and collaboratively worked on with editors, through a Google document.

- Google Alerts: You can use this service to set up an alert that will notify you when a word or phrase is mentioned on the web. In my case, I made an alert for both *My Virtual Girlfriend* and *My Virtual Boyfriend*. I have the alerts set up so that they send me an email once a day, notifying me of any blogs, reviews or even forum posts that mention my games. In the case of *My Virtual Girlfriend*, I initially released the game, but a Google alert notified me that a major Scandinavian news coverage site called "Spillmagasinet" wrote an article that pushed my ratings in Norway up to the #1 spot.

  I had no idea why this was happening until the alert notified me of the site, which was entirely in another language. I used Google Translate to read what was being said, then I promptly followed up with a press release about how the game hit #1 in Norway. That release caught the attention of gamepro.com, who then wrote an article as well as several other blog posts. The takeaway? Set this one up prior to the release of your game.

- Google Analytics: This is a web traffic monitoring tool. It offers analytics such as how many visitors come to your site each day along with their geographic data, type of web browsers, and the source of the traffic (the site they were on that led them to yours). This data can be especially valuable when trying to determine user demographics. It also helps you to determine the value of a particular site (i.e. who is sending traffic to your site) after a review.

In fact, when I run an advertising campaign on a site, I ask the site owner not to direct to my App store page, but instead, direct it to the App's website so I can measure how affective my ad is on that site. It allows me a means to measure how accurate it is against what the advertiser is claiming to have sent. The setup is fairly easy: you just insert a code snippet into the HTML on your webpage and you're up and running, when the google analytics bot verifies it. You will want to set this up synonymously with the official webpage for your app.

- Google Translate is also worth a mention because it can translate reviews from other countries if you're unfamiliar with the language. The accuracy will vary, but in any case it's not difficult to get the gist of what it's saying. It's also useful for translating iTunes app reviews you receive from players in other countries.

App Rankings And Analytics

There are some really great websites out there that offer tools for tracking ranking stats, from gathering geographical data of users to hourly rankings. The good news is that they range from free to cheap, and they are easy to set up.

- Appylzer is an online app rank monitoring tool. You can use its free service to monitor your rankings for different countries on a daily basis, or pay about $2.00 per month and you have access to hourly rankings and more. I've used this throughout development because of its simplicity and affordability—I've almost become addicted to this site and watching my rankings.

  The benefits with hourly rankings is that you can closely monitor sales, before the sale reports appear in iTunes connect. It allows you to see if a particular promotion you are running is working, and how well. It also feels really good to open the page and see you've reached a top spot in a particular country. I recommend this highly, especially for a newbie.

- AppAnnie is another useful site. They recently re-did their website with a host of new tools for developers. Entirely free, they allow you to check rankings from not only your apps, but all developer's apps and even the past history of rankings. To use it, just go to the website and type the name of your app in the search box on the right. A list of apps will come up—select the one you want to view and it will take you to the app details page. On the left side of that page, you'll find daily ranks and rank history, and features. I find the "highest ranks" particularly useful in that I can use that information on my app store page to impress potential buyers. Many developers do this, as a form of marketing to validate that the app is worthy for a consumer to make a purchase (i.e. "★ ★ ★ #1 App in the U.S. ★ ★ ★").

- Appfigures is probably the most comprehensive app monitoring and analytics tool available—it's what I currently use. If you're the type that likes to really dig into statistics, this one is for you. It can monitor rankings by the hour, profits from sales, iAds…it can even translate reviews for you. The only downside is that it requires access to your iTunes connect account directly. Although at first a bit reluctant to give that out, I've been using their service for year now and have had no security issues or problems. I really like the option to allow controlled access for others to see your stats, which comes in handy when dealing with vendors or sites that require proof in sales, such as was the case with FreeAppADay. The UI makes it a little overwhelming at first, but really, it's just presenting you with a lot of options — you will get to know the interface with time.

- xyologic I don't know how they are doing it, but I'm quite impressed. They offer statistics for downloads of any app in the app store, along with other mobile platforms. This can be either a good thing or a bad thing, depending on how you look at it. While you get to see exactly how other apps are doing, it also displays the information on your app to everyone else. By revealing this information, with some common sense and simple math, you can estimate revenues earned in iTunes for a particular app. This can be especially useful for developers in determining if an app idea is successful or not by evaluating similar apps to see how many downloads they've received.

Further Help

Task Managment: <u>Fellowstream</u> is an easy to use, web based, project collaboration and task management tool for developers. They offer a a simple tasking system for small to mid-sized teams. It's perfect for indie developers and it's even free for teams of two or less.

Testing: <u>Test flight</u> offers a Beta testing platform for mobile. It allows developers a method to distribute apps across multiple devices and get valuable feedback from various users.

App developer support groups: Below are a few developer related support groups that I found to be useful in connecting with other developers for an information exchange. For the sake of space I'm only listing out my top picks of each group here:

- Linkedin:

    - <u>Apple Mobile Dev Team</u>
    - <u>iPhone in touch</u>
    - <u>IPhone iPad group</u>

- App developer forums:

    - <u>iPhone dev SDK forum</u>
    - <u>Apple developer forums</u>
    - <u>TourchArcade – Developer forum</u>

- Game developer news and information:

    - <u>Gamastura.com</u> - the art and science of making games
    - <u>International Game Developers Association</u> - a good resource for new developers
    - <u>Gamedev.net</u> - Game developer news and community

- Game and app developer conventions:

    - <u>Game developers conference (GDC)</u> - a must attend event for app and game dev's, held annually in San Fransisco, CA, in or around early March.
    - <u>App developers conference</u> - a conference specific to those in the mobile apps industry
    - <u>E3 Expo</u> - not really a developer conference but a video game showcase and a must attend event. Several publishers and developers are there showcasing all their latest

products.

- **Development service marketplace:**

  - <u>App Tank</u> - post or bid on various app development projects.
  - <u>ODesk</u> - developers bid on projects or hire out an hourly rate contractor
  - <u>Elance</u> - developers for hire, or post your own service

- **Crowdsource funding:**

  - <u>Appbackr</u>- crowd source funding specific to mobile apps and games
  - <u>Kickstarter</u> - crowd source funding on all tops of projects (the biggest one out there)
  - <u>Appsfunder</u> - crowd funding for apps

- **App award sites:**

  - <u>Best App Ever</u>
  - <u>Apple Developer Awards</u>
  - <u>Appy Awards</u>
  - <u>Global Mobile Awards</u>
  - <u>Webby Awards</u>
  - <u>Mobile Premier Awards</u>

Chapter 7: Conclusion

Final Thoughts

Thank you for reading my book! I'm a game developer by trade, so I wasn't too sure how this would turn out. But being the optimist I am, I was willing to give it a shot. With the help of the editors at Hyperink, I think we managed to present this information in an effective manor and get it out there to the hands of developers looking for answers on the subject.

Through this process, I hope you have gained some insight into the world of iOS app marketing, and even some idea of who I am. I encourage you to download and play one of our flagship games — either My Virtual Girlfriend or My Virtual Boyfriend. It will give you a context for what I've been discussing in here.

The landscape of iOS app marketing changes constantly. New methods and opportunities spring up daily, and it's hard to keep on top of it all. My suggestion is to keep your eye out for new trends on the horizon. Watch other apps and developers who are successful in the iTunes app store market. Take the time to dissect what it is they are doing, that helps drive thier success. Do they reach out to the community through social networks? How often do they update? Are their games featured on any websites, and if so, which ones? Study them to find out what it is they are doing that helps to make them successful.

Apple maintains dominance in the market by offering a a simple yet stylish product line, known for the "wow" effect they create through an excellent user interface that consumers just can't get enough of. But one excellent method for learning all the latest trade secrets and trends of the industry is to attend the Game developers conference, held in San Fransisco every year around late February or early March. The GDC is great for developers and entrepreneurs alike. It offers a wealth of knowledge from the top industry experts across all disciplines, not just mobile. For an app developer, this is a must-attend venue because of the knowledge that can be obtained, as well as the fantastic networking opportunities. Just last year, Toucharcade.com threw a GDC after-party, and I got to meet the reviewers as well as several other top mobile app developers while I was there.

I wish you much happiness, growth and success as you embark on your journey. I've left my contact information below should you wish to connect with me.

Mike AmersonPresident, WET Productions Inc.

www.wetproductions.com Email: mike@wetproductions.com Linkedin:
http://www.linkedin.com/in/mikeamerson Twitter: http://www.twitter.com/polygrafix

Chapter 8: Bonus Materials

Web Resources

<u>Follow this link</u> to an online spreadsheet of my own creation, a one-stop resource for all your app marketing needs on the web. You'll find:

- 125+ iPhone app review sites
- 30+ Facebook groups and fan pages
- 15+ App and gaming forums
- 25+ YouTube reviewers
- 25+ Mobile marketing platforms

…and so much more. It serves as a reference of contacts and allows you to track which sites are covering your app, when you've last made contact with them and even a few direct reviewer contacts. I use this as a template to track coverage on my own apps. Because it's in spreadsheet format, you can sort by popularity or alphabetically. This is a huge timesaver when trying to organize and maintain a list of whom all you've been in contact with, or intend to contact regarding reviews.

High Concept Design Template

Where does one begin when designing a new app? Right here! Use this simple template to organize basic ideas to expand upon later. It's an easy basis to help you create your app or game design document. After completing the template, build it out into a full design document by adding the game flow and screenshots, and elaborate on the design elements.

Generic, High Concept Template (edit and use for your own purposes)

Title: World War 4

Platforms: iPhone, Android

Genre: Turn based strategy game

Category: Games/Strategy

Revenue Type: Free with in-app purchases

Development ETA: 6 months

Target Audience: Male, Ages 12-25

File Size Target: Under 20 MB

Reference: (List a couple links to other games that are similar in some aspect)

Header: (A single sentence that best describes the app/game) A futuristic military strategy game where you establish global dominance by defeating all other enemy nations.

Description: (A few paragraphs to paint a picture for the audience) It is 2023, You are the chief military commander of what's left of your nation after WW3 devastated the land in 2012. Just as the calm set in as we were picking up the pieces, tensions start to flare up with neighboring allies. One proclaims they are going to establish order by unifying the world under their regime, starting with your country! Now you must take what's left of your troops and defend your land. This is to be the beginning of what will become World War 4!

Features:

- 4 futuristic military branches to command
- 5 individual specialty squads within each branch
- Over 20+ hours single player campaign
- Multiplayer supports up to 10 players
- Turn based game play allows you to plan your attack
- Watch the fight! Epic battle cinematics in full 3D

Mockup: (Paste a simple mock-up image of the gameplay here)

Developer Notes:

- Game rewards players for daily active use, offering them special items.
- Most Items and powerups can be earned through progressive gameplay, but some can also be purchased for quick leveling up.
- Special "Rare" armors can be only acquired through gameplay by winning battles or purchased.

Version 1.0 Specs:

- iPad, 1st and 2nd generation. iPhone, 3G and up. iPod Touch, 3rd and 4th generation.
- Works only in landscape mode.
- Single-player support.
- Multi-player support.
- In-app purchase support.

Press Release Template

This is an actual Press Release of mine, sent out when we added zombies to our game (hey, it was before Halloween!). Go ahead and customize it for your own app.

For Immediate Release: Zombie dating comes to your iPhone

Summary:

Both My Virtual Girlfriend and My Virtual Boyfriend iphone apps have been updated in itunes which now includes Zombie girl and boy choices that you can date.

Las Vegas, Nevada – February 2nd, 2011 – WET Productions released a significant update to their hit IOS games: My Virtual Girlfriend and My Virtual Boyfriend, which now offers you choices of either Zombie girls or guys.

My Virtual Boyfriend and My Virtual Girlfriend are dating simulation games that feature a wide cast of characters with varying personalities and physical appearances. The goal of the game is getting your virtual companion to fall in love with you. This is achieved through conversation dialog and various other interactions you can do. My Virtual Girlfriend and My Virtual Boyfriend are universal apps that run on iPhone, iPod touch and iPad.

Updates 1.6 Includes:

Zombie Girlfriends and Boyfriends A character editor Additional Halloween themed content General Improvements and performance enhancements

Device Requirements: iPhone, iPad and iPod Touch 72.5 MB

Pricing and Availability: My Virtual Boyfriend and Girlfriend are available worldwide, exclusively through the app store on iTunes, priced at $.99. Review copies are available upon request.

My Virtual Girlfriend in iTunes: http://itunes.apple.com/app/myvirtualgirlfriend/id369849199

My Virtual Boyfriend in

iTunes: http://itunes.apple.com/app/myvirtualboyfriend/id441072365?mt=8

Mike Amerson President 702-460-0428 mike@wetproductions.com
http://www.wetproductions.com **###**

Which Friends Will Receive Your Gift?

Thanks for purchasing a Hyperink book!

As a huge thank you, and because books are better when you can talk about 'em with friends, here are 5 free copies:

CLICK HERE TO GIFT THEM NOW!

Join 1000s of other readers of **IOS App Marketing**.

Simply follow these 3 steps:

Step 1. Click this link

Step 2. Fill out your email

Step 3. Add the emails of up to 5 friends

That's it. Soon after, your friends will receive a special link to download **IOS App Marketing**.

We take your privacy very seriously, and we will never share your email with any 3rd parties.

Please email me at brandon@hyperink.com if you have questions or the promo doesn't work for whatever reason. Thanks!

-Brandon "That Marketing Guy From Hyperink"

P.S. We hope your friends enjoy it. It'd be awesome if you could follow us on Twitter and Facebook!

About The Publisher

Hyperink is the easiest way for anyone to publish a beautiful, high-quality book.

We work closely with subject matter experts to create each book. We cover topics ranging from higher education to job recruiting, from Android apps marketing to barefoot running.

If you have interesting knowledge that people are willing to pay for, especially if you've already produced content on the topic, please reach out to us! There's no writing required and it's a unique opportunity to build your own brand and earn royalties.

Hyperink is based in SF and actively hiring people who want to shape publishing's future. Email us if you'd like to meet our team!

Note: If you're reading this book in print or on a device that's not web-enabled, **please email** books@hyperinkpress.com with the title of this book in the subject line. We'll send you a PDF copy, so you can access all of the great content we've included as clickable links.

READERS WHO ENJOYED THIS BOOK ALSO ENJOYED!

The Best Book On Marketing Your Android App

Making no money on your Android app? An independent developer who successfully makes $100K+ a year selling Android apps shares his marketing secrets to high rankings, maximizing revenue, and satisfied buyers!

$25

BUY NOW

How To Get The Most From Your Kindle

$3.99

BUY NOW

The Best Book on Marketing Your Android App

$25.00

BUY NOW

Printed in Great Britain
by Amazon.co.uk, Ltd.,
Marston Gate.